The Baby Gourmet Cookbook

By
Mary Bayley Fisk

Illustrations by
Susan Perl

The Baby Gourmet Cookbook
Recipes © 1975, 1978 Determined Productions, Inc.
Illustrations © 1975, 1978 Susan Perl
Published by Determined Productions, Inc.
Box 2150, San Francisco, CA 94126
World Rights Reserved

Enlarged Edition. First Printing May, 1978
Library of Congress Card Catalog Number: 77-90651
ISBN 0-915696-09-6
Printed in the United States of America

For my own Baby Gourmet Rebekah

Contents

𝕴ntroduction

Cooking is creative. Eating is a pleasure. Cooking for a baby is both. You can feed your baby with fresh fruit and combinations of fish, meat and vegetables as tasty as they are nutritious. Baby food need not be dull or unappetizing. To prepare it well is work for the cook, but it can be satisfying work and it's less expensive than the lazy alternative of paying for jars, cans and advertising.

Babies are amazingly discriminating and they do respond to dishes that are prepared with thought and affection. Plan your shopping, storing and preparation of food carefully. Keep learning all you can about good nutrition and try to lay the foundation during the baby's first years for a lifetime of happy, healthful eating pleasures.

Bon petit appetit!

Food for Thought

1. Each baby is an individual. Likes and dislikes appear early in life. Respect them.

2. Start feeding solid foods whenever you and your doctor decide the time has come. Three months is usually a good time to start them.

3. Offer one new food at a time. Try it for a few days. If the baby refuses it consistently, give up. Try again at a later time.

4. Try to create a well-balanced diet but keep the servings small.

5. Be patient. Never force food. Let the baby decide how much is enough. Follow this general guide for the maximum amount of each food:

3 to 6 months	two tablespoons
6 to 9 months	four tablespoons
9 months and up	one-half cup

6. Discuss allergic reactions with your doctor, then watch for them.

7. Do not accustom your baby to adult preferences for controversial amounts of salt and sugar.

8. Read leading authorities on baby foods and feeding, but keep in mind that you know your baby better than they do.

Food Storage

Baby foods made from fruits and vegetables should be refrigerated no more than three days. Foods prepared with milk for a very young baby should be kept only one day. Bacteria grow quickly in milk. Never keep soup broth more than 3 days unless you bring it to a good boil every third day.

Make up food and pour it into an ice-cube tray. Freeze it immediately to retain valuable nutrients. When it is frozen, pack cubes in single portions in plastic cooking bags and return to freezer. Just before feeding time, pop a bag into boiling water for a few minutes.

Food Additives

Many food additives such as preservatives, stabilizers, hydrogenated fats, artificial colors, flavors, and sweeteners are controversial and may be harmful to your baby's health. Preparation of baby foods demands careful reading of labels. Try to use ingredients that are natural and unrefined. Some additives and terms used that are currently controversial and should probably be avoided are: BHA, BHT, methyl cellulose, carboxymethyl cellulose, hydrogenated or partially hardened oils, sodium nitrate and sodium nitrite, MSG, artificial colors, flavors and sweeteners. Keep track of controversial additives through newspapers and magazines. If in doubt, don't buy. Select the best and safest foods for a happy and healthy baby.

Food Preparation

In testing recipes with a blender we have found that you have to use your own judgment about amounts of time for blending, since blending for a longer time on a lower speed will produce the same result as blending for a shorter time on a higher speed. Ingredients do not always have the same consistency. Eggs vary in size, vegetables may not be as crisp as they should be, and the amount of liquid determines the consistency. You may have to experiment to find the consistency your baby likes best. You may want to start with a thin mixture and try thicker ones after the baby is accustomed to the taste and texture of the food.

Most of the recipes in this book are for small amounts of food, enough for 1 or 2 servings, except where these amounts seemed impractical and where it seemed convenient to make and store larger amounts.

Beginners
(three to six months)

At three months your baby will begin to eat cereal, vegetables and fruits. Then, fish and meat can be introduced. Serve each kind of food separately at first, then mix them together. Many combinations are good, but some are tastier than others. Recipes for our favorites follow. You will need a fine strainer, a food mill, a blender, or one of the new food processing machines for preparing fruits, vegetables, fish and meat.

MILK

If you start your baby early on home-fortified milk, you will never need to worry about nutritional lack when you are rushed for time or too tired to cook. If you breast feed your baby, try this for supplementary bottles.

1. Put the following ingredients into a blender:

  1 can (6-oz.) frozen orange juice concentrate
  2 tablespoons soy oil
  1 teaspoon kelp powder
1½ to 2 cups whole milk
  ½ cup brewer's or nutritional yeast

Blend thoroughly and pour into a 6-cup container.

2. Put these ingredients into a blender:

  ½ cup wheat germ
  1 tablespoon lecithin
  1 to 2 tablespoons blackstrap molasses
    Milk enough to fill blender to within an inch of the top

Blend thoroughly and add to first mixture.

3. Stir until mixtures are well blended. Store in refrigerator.

EGG YOLK

Your baby should be ready to eat egg yolk at about four months. Here are three ways to prepare it:

1. Remove yolk from a hard-cooked egg. Press through a fine strainer. Mix with boiled water to form a paste.

2. Remove egg yolk from a hard-cooked egg. Crumble it. Add it to other food.

3. Feed yolk of soft-cooked egg with a spoon, offering just a taste to start with, then more.

Gradually increase the amount of yolk until the baby can eat a whole one. At about six months, you can introduce the egg white. Increase the egg white until the baby is eating the whole egg.

JUICE

Always give your baby pure, unsweetened fruit and vegetable juices. Prepare juice from fresh fruits and vegetables if you can, otherwise choose from the many canned or frozen ones available. Citrus juices such as orange, grapefruit and lemon are high in vitamin C. Apricot, papaya and mango juices are high in vitamin A.

Prepare vegetable juices by cooking vegetables in water. Carrot juice is high in vitamin A and the green, leafy vegetables are high in vitamin and mineral amounts. Carrot and celery juice are good ones to start with.

CEREAL

Packaged baby cereals are enriched with vitamins and iron. Mix them with formula or instant milk and boiling water. Increase the strength of the milk and the thickness of the mixture as the baby gets used to it. For variety, sweeten it with honey, brown sugar, or, best of all, a fruit puree.

FRUIT

Canned fruit is the easiest to prepare. Pour off the syrup, then puree the fruit or put it through a strainer. Fresh fruit is best, but more work. It must be peeled, cored or pitted and sliced. It should then be simmered until just tender, in a small amount of water, sweetened to taste and strained.

VEGETABLES

Deep green and deep yellow vegetables are the most nutritious but you can start with almost any vegetable. Cook fresh vegetables until tender, in a small amount of water, reserving the cooking water. Strain or puree the vegetable, then mix it with cooking water until you have the consistency you want. Or, better still, prepare the vegetable with milk to make it sweeter and more nourishing. Put the cooked, strained vegetable into a saucepan with milk in the proportion of four parts vegetable to one part milk and simmer for a few minutes. Be sure to strain all vegetables containing seeds.

FISH

Fish is a highly nutritious and delicious alternative to meat. It is easy for babies to chew and swallow and should be served at least once a week. Buy fresh fish whenever you can. A large filet can be cut up into chunks and frozen in baby-size portions for later use.

To prepare fish, simply steam, bake or poach it until it is tender but not mushy. Fish is done when it flakes easily when tested with a fork. Cool slightly, then carefully flake it with your fingers to check for bones and scales to discard. Combine 4 parts of the cooked fish with 1 part of cooking liquid or milk, put into a blender and blend to the consistency your baby prefers.

MEAT

Take a good quality, lean meat such as steak or lamb and scrape with a spoon. Put the scraped meat into a custard cup or small jar. Put the cup into a pan of water. The water should come halfway up the sides of the jar. Heat the water to boiling and boil until the meat changes color.

Another good way to prepare meat is with a blender. Combine four parts of any cooked meat with one part boiled water, vegetable cooking water or tomato juice.

Baby Soups

Homemade soups can contribute important nutrients to your baby's diet. They are easy to make, can be frozen in small or large amounts for later use, and can be served to the whole family.

Directions follow for making a broth which can be used as it is, as a base for cream soups, and as the basic liquid for many of the recipes in this book.

BROTH

You can make this with meat, poultry or fish bones and it is worthwhile to make a sizeable amount since it can be used in so many ways and since it can be frozen in various quantities.

> 2 quarts of water
> Meat, poultry or fish bones
> 2 tablespoons vinegar
> 2 teaspoons salt

Simmer for 2 hours. Add an assortment of fresh or leftover vegetables. Leeks, carrots, potatoes, celery and parsley are a good combination for a real "pot au feu" flavor.

Cover and simmer for another hour. Strain through a coarse strainer or colander. Discard bones and vegetables. Chill. Skim off fat. If stock is not to be used immediately, heat to the boiling point, then pour into storage containers for freezing. Serve it as it is or use it as a base for vegetable, meat, rice or noodle soup.

CREAM SOUP

Put 1 cup of broth into a saucepan. Add ¼ cup meat or vegetables and cook covered until tender. Put into a blender. Add enough milk or cream to thin to desired consistency. Reheat if necessary, and serve.

Baby Mushes

BEANS & HAM

¼ cup cooked green beans
¼ cup chopped baked or boiled ham
2 tablespoons vegetable water

Combine ingredients. Put through a strainer or blend in a blender.

LIVER & BACON

¼ cup minced cooked liver
¼ cup cooked green peas
1 slice crisp crumbled bacon
2 tablespoons vegetable water

Combine ingredients. Put through a strainer or blend in a blender.

SPINACH

½ cup cooked chopped spinach
2 tablespoons milk
1 hard-cooked egg yolk

Mash ingredients together. Put through strainer or blend.

SWEET POTATO OR SQUASH

½ cup cooked sweet potato or squash
2 tablespoons milk
1 teaspoon brown sugar
Sliver of butter

Mash ingredients together until smooth.

LAMB

¼ cup minced cooked lamb
2 tablespoons cooked green peas
2 tablespoons mashed cooked carrots
2 tablespoons vegetable water

Combine ingredients. Put through strainer or blend in a blender.

BEEF & PEA

½ cup cooked fresh peas
2 tablespoons ground beef sautéed lightly in butter
1 tablespoon vegetable water or milk
  Salt to taste

Combine all ingredients and put through strainer or blend in a blender.

POTATO & HAM

⅓ cup diced cooked potato
2 tablespoons finely chopped ham
1 or more tablespoons milk
  Sliver of butter
  Salt to taste

Combine all ingredients and put through strainer or blend in a blender.

CHICKEN

¼ cup chopped cooked chicken
2 tablespoons mashed cooked carrots
2 tablespoons cooked green peas
2 tablespoons milk

Combine ingredients. Put through strainer or blend in a blender.

PORK

¼ cup minced cooked pork
2 tablespoons mashed cooked sweet potato
2 tablespoons chopped cooked spinach
2 tablespoons milk or vegetable water
  Pinch of salt

Cook vegetables and reserve cooking liquid. Combine ingredients. Add liquid. Put through strainer or blend in a blender.

CELERY & BEEF

½ cup finely diced cooked celery
  (Be sure to remove all strings from celery before cooking.)
2 tablespoons ground beef sautéed lightly in butter
1 or more tablespoons milk or vegetable water
  Salt to taste

Combine ingredients. Put through strainer or blend in a blender.

CARROT

¼ cup cooked carrot
¼ cup cooked potato
1 hard-cooked egg yolk
2 tablespoons vegetable water

Combine cooked vegetables and egg yolk. Mash well with a fork. Add liquid until of desired consistency.

BEEF

¼ cup minced cooked beef
¼ cup chopped cooked sweet onions
2 tablespoons milk
Pinch of salt

Combine beef, onions and milk. Put through strainer or blend. Add salt.

FISH

¼ cup minced cooked fish
¼ cup mashed potato
3 tablespoons hot milk
¼ teaspoon grated Parmesan cheese

Combine ingredients. Cook and stir for a few minutes. Put through a strainer or blend in a blender.

AVOCADO

3 tablespoons mashed avocado
¼ cup creamed cottage cheese
¼ teaspoon lemon juice
Pinch of salt

Combine ingredients. Put through a strainer or blend in a blender.

MUSHROOM

2 tablespoons minced cooked mushroooms
½ cup chopped cooked spinach
1 hard-cooked egg yolk
  Pinch of garlic salt
2 tablespoons milk

Cook mushrooms in milk for a few minutes. Mash egg yolk and add. Add spinach and garlic salt. Heat together. Put through a strainer or blend in a blender.

ZUCCHINI & CHICKEN

½ cup finely sliced zucchini
1 small, thin slice of onion
2 tablespoons finely chopped cooked chicken
1 teaspoon chicken broth or vegetable water
  Sliver of butter
  Salt to taste

Cook zucchini and onion together. Add rest of ingredients and put through a strainer or blend in a blender.

SWEET BEEF

¼ cup cooked, chopped beef
¼ cup meat juice or milk
1 heaping tablespoon raisins
3 tablespoons milk

Soak raisins in milk for at least an hour. Mix all ingredients together and puree in a blender until smooth.

BROCCOLI BEEF

¼ cup cooked broccoli
¼ cup cooked, minced beef
2 tablespoons milk
Pinch of salt

Combine ingredients. Mash with a fork or puree in a blender. Serve warm.

TONGUE & CARROT

¼ cup boiled tongue
¼ cup carrot puree or cooked carrots
2 tablespoons tomato juice
3 tablespoons tongue broth or milk

Combine all ingredients. Put through a strainer or into a blender. Adjust consistency to taste.

PEANUT BANANA CREAM

½ peeled banana
1 tablespoon cream cheese
2 tablespoons peanut butter

Mash banana with a fork. Add cream cheese and peanut butter. Stir until smooth. Thin with small amount of milk if too sticky.

APPLE PUDDING

1 large eating apple, peeled, cored
Pinch of cinnamon
2 tablespoons sour cream or plain yogurt
1 tablespoon wheat germ

Cut apple into chunks and cook in a small amount of water until soft. Sprinkle lightly with cinnamon. Puree all ingredients in a blender or put apple through a strainer after it is cooked, then add other ingredients and stir until smooth.

Beginning Gourmets

GREEN BEAN & CARROT SOUP

1 cup carrots, cut into chunks
1 cup green beans, cut into pieces
4 cups water

Combine ingredients. Simmer uncovered until vegetables are tender and about half of the water has evaporated. Remove from heat. Put vegetables into a blender with 1 cup of the remaining cooking water. Blend. (Add more water for a thinner soup.) Makes about 1½ cups.

RATATOUILLE

2 tablespoons each of the following
vegetables, peeled and chopped:
    Zucchini
    Onion
    Eggplant
    Fresh tomato
1 tablespoon cooking oil
    Salt to taste

Heat oil in frying pan. Add vegetables. Cover. Cook until soft. Add salt. Put through a strainer or blend in a blender. Serve hot or cold.

VEGETABLE OR FRUIT SOUFFLÉS

⅓ cup vegetable puree (carrot, green bean
    squash, asparagus tip, spinach)
OR
⅓ cup fruit puree (apple, pear, apricot,
    peach, plum)
1 egg, separated
2 tablespoons evaporated milk
    Butter

Put puree, egg yolk and evaporated milk into a small bowl or measuring cup. Beat with an egg beater until frothy. Beat the egg white to stiff peaks. Fold egg white into puree mixture. Spoon into 3 small custard cups and bake 20 minutes at 300.°

EARLY RISER'S RICE

1 tablespoon raw rice
½ cup chopped carrot, apple or green beans
½ teaspoon salt
3 cups water

Put all ingredients into a saucepan and boil until soft. Pour through a strainer reserving liquid. Puree rice mixture in a blender, adding liquid until you have the consistency you want. Add a little sugar if you like.

CORNED BEEF HASH

½ cup diced cooked corned beef
½ cup diced boiled potato
¼ cup diced cooked carrots
2 to 3 tablespoons potato water

Cook potato and carrots, reserving water. Combine ingredients. Put through a strainer or blend in a blender. For babies six months or more, combine ingredients and put through a meat grinder.

TUNA CUPCAKES

1 (7-oz.) can tuna fish
1 egg
1 slice whole-wheat bread
½ cup milk

Put all ingredients into a blender and blend until smooth. Pour into buttered custard cups or muffin tins with paper cupcake liners. Set cups in a baking pan. Fill pan with hot water until water comes halfway up sides of cups. Bake 30 minutes at 325° or until mixture is set. Makes 6 to 10 cupcakes. You may substitute any meat, vegetable or combination of the two for the tuna. Cupcakes can be frozen.

SMOOTH SALMON LOAF

1 (7-oz.) can salmon
1 egg
1 thick slice bread, cubed
½ cup milk
   Dash powdered onion
½ teaspoon chopped parsley
¼ teaspoon dill weed
2 heaping tablespoons lemon yogurt

Discard salmon skin and bones. Put all ingredients into a blender and puree until smooth. (If you do not have a blender, make crumbs out of the bread, mix all ingredients and put them through a food mill or mash and beat them with a wooden spoon until blended.) You will have about 2 cups of mixture. Pour into a buttered baking dish or make individual servings by pouring mixture into a muffin tin lined with paper cupcake liners. Bake at 325° for 30 minutes. Serve hot or cold. You may freeze this before or after baking.

Topping: (optional) Make a thin cream sauce by melting 1 tablespoon of butter, adding 1 tablespoon of flour and stirring well. Add 1 cup of milk slowly and stir and cook until smooth. Add salt to taste if you wish. Spoon over slices of salmon loaf.

ASPARAGUS ASPIC

1 cup canned asparagus
2 tablespoons chopped onion (optional)
1 teaspoon sugar
1 tablespoon minced green pepper
1 cup vegetable water
1 tablespoon gelatin, soaked in ½ cup
   cold water

Drain asparagus and reserve water. Simmer onion and green pepper until soft. Combine all ingredients except gelatin and put through a strainer or blend in a blender. Combine strained mixture with gelatin and heat and stir until gelatin is dissolved. Pour into small jars or custard cups. Chill. Makes about 2 cups.

BEET ASPIC

Substitute canned beets for asparagus.

CARROT ASPIC

Substitute cooked carrots for asparagus. Add ¼ cup chopped celery and a pinch of dill weed.

TOMATO ASPIC

(1 tablespoon of unflavored gelatin turns 2 cups of liquid to a gelatin.)

- ½ cup cold water
- 1 tablespoon unflavored gelatin
- 2 cups tomato juice
- ⅛ teaspoon celery salt
- 1 tablespoon lemon juice
  Dash of Worcestershire sauce

Sprinkle gelatin on the ½ cup of cold water and set aside. Combine tomato juice, celery salt, lemon juice and Worcestershire sauce in a saucepan and heat to boiling. Simmer 3 to 5 minutes. Add gelatin. Stir until gelatin is dissolved. Pour into buttered mold or bowl. Chill in refrigerator overnight.

APPLESAUCE

3 tart cooking apples
¼ cup water
   Pinch of salt
3 tablespoons sugar

Peel and slice apples. Combine with water and salt and simmer until almost soft. Add sugar. Stir and simmer for a few more minutes. Strain through fine sieve. For variety add ½ teaspoon lemon juice or a sprinkle of ground cinnamon or nutmeg.

PEACH SAUCE

Substitute 3 fresh peaches for apples.

APRICOT SAUCE

Substitute 4 apricots for apples.

PEAR SAUCE

3 ripe fresh pears
¼ cup water
1 to 2 tablespoons sugar
Lemon juice
Nutmeg

Peel, core and slice pears. Combine with water in a saucepan and simmer until soft. Add sugar. Stir and simmer a couple of minutes more. Strain through a sieve. Sprinkle with drops of lemon juice and fine grated nutmeg.

BANANA SUPRÊME

2 to 3 bananas
3 tablespoons apricot jam
1 tablespoon cornstarch
1 cup milk

Mash bananas. Add jam. Mix milk and cornstarch in a saucepan. Cook and stir until thick and pour over banana mixture. Stir and chill.

ORANGE PUDDING

½ cup sugar
2 tablespoons flour
⅔ cup milk
2 beaten egg yolks
Juice of 1 orange (about ⅓ cup)
2 beaten egg whites

Mix in order given. Pour into custard cups. Set in pan of hot water with water three-quarters of the way up sides of cups. Bake at 325° for 30 minutes. For LEMON PUDDING, substitute lemon juice for orange. For GRAPE NUT PUDDING for babies six months or more, add ¼ cup Grape Nuts.

ORANGE-JUICE YOGURT

3 teaspoons frozen orange juice concentrate
4 tablespoons plain yogurt

Combine ingredients. Beat with an egg beater until smooth.

FRUIT-FLAVORED YOGURT

Mix equal amounts of plain yogurt and fruit puree.

FRUIT-JUICE JELLO

1½ teaspoons plain gelatin (½ packet)
1 cup apple juice (or any natural fruit juice except fresh or frozen pineapple)
2 teaspoons honey (optional)
Juice of ½ lemon

Soak gelatin in ½ cup of apple juice for 5 minutes. Heat until gelatin dissolves. Add remaining ingredients and stir well. Cool slightly. Pour into small paper cups. Chill until set.

CRÈME CARAMELETTE

Make a caramel sauce by putting ½ cup sugar and ¼ cup water into a heavy saucepan and cooking until sugar turns syrupy and light brown. Put this in the bottom of the buttered custard cups. Pour custard on top, then bake.

Custard:
2 cups milk, scalded and slightly cooled
¼ cup sugar
2 beaten eggs
Pinch of salt
½ teaspoon vanilla

Add sugar and salt to beaten eggs. Add scalded milk slowly, stirring until sugar is dissolved. Add vanilla. Pour into buttered custard cups. Set in pan of hot water with water three-quarters of the way up sides of cups. Bake at 325° for about 45 minutes or until a knife blade inserted in the center comes out clean.

CRANBERRY-BANANA DRINK

⅓ cup cranberry juice
½ small banana, cut up

Put ingredients into a blender and mix, or put the banana through a fine strainer, and whip into cranberry juice. For ORANGE-BANANA DRINK, substitute the juice of one orange for cranberry juice. Put orange juice through a strainer, then add banana and strain together with juice.

COLD OATMEAL CREAM

1 cup baby oatmeal
½ cup milk
1 beaten egg
2 tablespoons honey
1 tablespoon gelatin, soaked in ¼ cup cold water
½ cup heavy cream
Fruit puree

Put all ingredients except cream and fruit into a saucepan and stir over very low heat until gelatin is dissolved. Remove from heat. Whip cream into soft peaks. Fold into oatmeal mixture. Cool. Serve plain or topped with any fruit puree.

Intermediate Gourmets
(six to nine months)

You can begin to vary the consistency of foods when your baby is about six months old. Use the same recipes and foods you have been using, but start to chop, crumble, shred and lump instead of strain. Begin offering finger foods.

GRANDMA'S SOUP

¼ pound round steak
1 stalk celery, chopped
1 carrot, chopped
1 tablespoon chopped onion
1 tablespoon rice
Salt to taste

Cut meat into slivers. Put ingredients into a saucepan with about 2 cups of water. Bring to a boil. Reduce heat and simmer until vegetables are barely tender.

CHICKEN SOUP

Chicken neck, back and giblets
2 carrots
2 stalks celery
1 small onion
¼ cup green peas
¼ cup green beans

Put chicken into a pan with water to cover and one cup more. Bring to a boil. Reduce heat and simmer for about 45 minutes, covered. Cool in refrigerator and then remove congealed fat. Chop the vegetables and add to broth. Cook until the vegetables are tender. Remove the chicken, cut off the meat and put it back into the soup. Serve broth and vegetables separately if you wish.

BEAN CURD SOUP

1½ cups chicken broth or beef bouillon
2 one-inch cubes bean curd

Bean curd, that bland custard-like Oriental product made from soy-beans, is a delicious addition to plain soup. Drop the cubes into boiling broth and simmer for about 5 minutes. The baby can eat the bean curd after the broth is eaten. (Makes 2 servings.)

BABY BORSCHT

½ cup cooked, mashed beets
1 tablespoon sour cream
1 teaspoon butter

Melt butter in saucepan. Add beets and heat. Add sour cream. Mash to desired consistency. Serve hot or cold.

LENTILS FOR LITTLE ONES

3 cups water
1 teaspoon salt
½ cup lentils
1 cup chopped ham or beef
3 small carrots, scraped, chopped
1 small onion, peeled, chopped

Put all ingredients into a soup pot, bring to a boil, turn down heat, cover and simmer for 1½ hours. Put through a strainer, reserving liquid. Put lentil mixture into a blender and puree, adding as much soup liquid as you like until you get the consistency you want. If you keep the soup quite thick, your baby can lick it off a spoon. Makes about 4 cups of soup. Freezes well.

EGG DROP SOUP

1 cup minced, cooked chicken breast
   or minced, cooked pork
3 cups chicken broth
1 tablespoon cornstarch (dissolved in
      2 tablespoons cold water)
1 egg, beaten
   Dash of soy sauce

Put chicken or pork and broth into a saucepan and bring to a boil. Dissolve the cornstarch in the water and add, stirring constantly until well blended. Pour beaten egg into soup in steady stream while stirring. Add soy sauce. Cool slightly and serve.

FIRST SALAD

2 teaspoons grated apple
2 teaspoons grated carrot
1 teaspoon wheat germ
⅓ cup vanilla or lemon yogurt

Combine all ingredients. Mix well and serve.

FISH FILET

Place a small filet of sole, flounder, or any non-oily white fish in ½ cup milk and simmer gently for about 5 minutes. Spoon-feed the broth, but flake the fish with your fingers, being very careful to inspect each piece for bones and scales, before feeding it to the baby.

Alternate method: Bake in a 350° oven for about 10 minutes in a small ovenproof dish with a bit of butter and grated cheese sprinkled on top.

QUESADILLA

1 flour tortilla
2 slices Monterey Jack cheese

Put the tortilla in a frying pan or on a griddle over low heat. Put cheese slices on half of the tortilla. When the tortilla is soft and slightly puffy, fold it over the cheese. Cook until cheese is melted, turning once. Cut into pie-shaped wedges.

BABY EGGS BENEDICT

1 egg
1 tablespoon cream cheese
2 tablespoons chopped ham
4 slices bread

Puree the egg and cheese in a blender. Cut bread into 4 crustless 3-inch rounds with a cookie cutter or glass rim. Butter two custard cups and put 1 round of bread in the bottom of each cup. Pour half the egg mixture over the bread in one cup and the other half over the bread in the other cup. Sprinkle the ham on top of the egg mixture and top each serving with a second bread round. Bake for 10 minutes in a 325° oven. Remove from cups and invert on a plate.

COTTAGE EGGS

1 tablespoon small curd cottage
  cheese
1 egg, beaten until light
1 slice crisp bacon, crumbled or
  1 tablespoon finely chopped
  cooked ham or pork sausage
  Salt to taste

Stir cottage cheese into beaten egg and mix well. Add meat. Stir over low heat or in top of double boiler until eggs are set. Add salt if you wish. If you wish to omit the meat, add a bit of minced parsley to the egg mixture before cooking.

POPEYE PANCAKES

2 tablespoons frozen chopped spinach
½ cup milk
1 egg
1 tablespoon oil
½ cup flour
2 tablespoons instant non-fat dry milk
1 teaspoon baking soda
1 teaspoon sugar

Cut 2 one-inch cubes from a frozen block of spinach and return the rest to the freezer. Defrost and squeeze out excess water. Mix flour, dry milk, soda and sugar together. Add milk, egg and oil and stir until mixed. Add spinach to batter and stir until mixed. Drop by tablespoonsful onto oiled griddle and bake until lightly browned on one side. Turn and brown the other side. Serve plain or with syrup or with a sour cream topping sprinkled with powdered sugar.

FRENCH TOAST

1 egg, lightly beaten
¼ teaspoon salt
⅓ cup milk
Bread slices
Butter for browning

Put egg, salt and milk into a shallow bowl and beat lightly. Trim crusts from bread and cut into rings with a doughnut cutter. Dip in mixture to coat both sides of bread. Heat butter in small frying pan and brown the bread on both sides. Spread with a little bit of clear red jelly.

GRANOLA WAFFLES

¾ cup flour
1 teaspoon baking powder
1 egg, beaten
¾ cup milk
1 tablespoon oil
½ cup granola, powdered in a blender
1 teaspoon sugar (optional)

Mix dry ingredients together. Stir in liquid ingredients. Bake in an oiled waffle iron. Serve whole or cut into small pieces.

GRANOLA PANCAKES

¾ cup flour
1 teaspoon baking powder
1 egg, beaten
1 cup milk
1 tablespoon melted butter
½ cup granola, powdered in a blender

Mix ingredients in order given. Drop by tablespoonsful on hot griddle and bake until bubbly on top. Turn and brown on other side.

MEATBALLS FOR FUSSY EATERS

Roll a good quality hamburger into very small meatballs, about ½-inch in diameter. Put into the pan equal amounts of catsup and brown sugar and a dash of Worcestershire sauce. Add meatballs and cook until brown. Good for babies who like to feed themselves.

LIVER

Fry liver very quickly in a little bacon fat, so that the liver is soft and pink inside. For a small piece, it should require only a minute on each side. Chop into bits or little strips or mash with a fork.

LIVER & RICE

1 small piece calf's liver, minced
1 teaspoon oil
1 to 2 tablespoons rice
1 cup water

Sauté liver in oil. Cook rice in water until tender. Drain rice and combine with liver. Makes 1 serving. Veal and lamb are also good with rice but should be ground before browning.

LIVER CEREAL

2 tablespoons wheat cereal, such as farina
½ cup milk
2 tablespoons chopped calf's liver
1 teaspoon butter

Brown liver in butter, then mash with a fork. Heat milk to boiling point and add cereal 1 spoonful at a time stirring until thick. Mix cooked cereal and liver together. Cereal is a good substitute for potato or bread. Try it with other meats and vegetables if the baby likes it.

GROUND BEEF

Brown a small amount of good quality ground beef in a little oil for a minute or two. Keep the meat medium rare so it won't be tough. Mix with a favorite vegetable and serve.

CREAMED CAULIFLOWER

1 tablespoon butter
1 tablespoon flour
1 cup milk
1 teaspoon sugar
1½ cups finely chopped cooked cauliflower
   Salt to taste

Melt butter. Stir in flour. Add milk slowly, stirring until smooth. Add sugar, cauliflower, and salt. Simmer for 5 minutes. For young babies, put cauliflower through a sieve before adding to sauce.

GREENS & CARROTS

¼ cup greens (beet, spinach, chard,
   collard or mustard)
½ cup raw sliced carrots
¼ cup water
1 tablespoon brown sugar
1 tablespoon cornstarch

Put all ingredients into a blender. Blend to desired consistency. Pour into saucepan. Stir over heat about 5 minutes. (To prepare without blending, cook greens and carrots and combine with remaining ingredients. Simmer, strain and serve.)

BACON TOMATO TREAT

3 strips crumbled crisp bacon
¼ cup water
1 small apple, peeled and cut into chunks
1 large fresh tomato, peeled, cut into pieces

Put into blender and blend. Thicken with baby cereal if you like.

CHICKEN & MACARONI

¼ cup shredded, cooked chicken
¼ cup cooked macaroni
4 tablespoons milk or chicken broth
  Pinch of thyme
  Salt to taste

Combine all ingredients. Put through a sieve or puree in a blender. This will be a slightly lumpy dish. Pour into a saucepan, heat and serve.

MACARONI À LA CRÈME

½ cup macaroni
1 tablespoon butter
2 teaspoons flour
¾ cup milk
  Salt and pepper to taste
½ cup grated cheese

Cook macaroni in 4 cups of boiling water until tender (10 to 15 minutes). Melt butter in heavy saucepan. Remove from heat. Stir in flour. Return to heat. Add milk slowly, stirring and cooking until smooth. Add cheese. Drain macaroni and put into a dish. Pour hot sauce over it and serve immediately. If desired, mash the macaroni after it is cooked. Makes about 1 cup.

FROZEN PUMPKIN YUMMY

1 (5½-oz.) can evaporated milk
1 cup cooked pumpkin
¼ cup honey
¼ teaspoon cinnamon
   (or ¼ teaspoon pumpkin pie spice)
¼ teaspoon ginger
   (or ¼ teaspoon pumpkin pie spice)
   Pinch of salt
½ cup plain yogurt

Combine all ingredients except yogurt and mix until smooth. Put into freezer-proof dish and freeze until half frozen. Beat the yogurt until it is smooth and stir into the pumpkin mixture. Freeze.

SPICY PEARS

1 small canned pear half, chopped
1 tablespoon small curd cottage cheese
1 teaspoon pear juice
Cinnamon and nutmeg to taste
Fresh lemon juice to taste

Combine all ingredients and chill slightly before serving.

ORANGE MILK ICE

¼ cup orange juice
1 tablespoon lemon juice
1 cup sugar
2 cups milk

Mix all ingredients together. Put into freezer-proof dish and freeze until mushy. Stir thoroughly with a spoon to make it fluffy. Freeze until solid.

FRUIT CUSTARD

1 cup milk
1 tablespoon sugar
1 tablespoon cornstarch
1 egg, beaten
1 teaspoon vanilla
  Pinch of cinnamon
½ peeled banana

Scald milk and set aside. Put sugar, cornstarch and egg into a heavy saucepan and mix well. Add milk and cook over low heat, stirring constantly until thick. Remove from heat. Add vanilla and cinnamon. Pour into small cups if you want to serve it plain, or put the custard into a blender with ½ a banana or ½ cup of other fruit and blend until smooth. Chill.

COTTAGE CHEESE PIE

2 eggs
1 pint creamed cottage cheese
1 teaspoon salt
1 teaspoon baking powder
2 tablespoons flour
1 cup grated cheddar cheese
1 slice whole wheat bread, made into crumbs
½ cup cooked, chopped ham or crisp bacon
  bits (optional)

Mix all ingredients together in a baking dish. Stir until well mixed. Bake 25 to 30 minutes at 350°.

GRAHAM CRACKER CAKE

20 whole graham crackers
1 cup nuts
⅓ cup flour
2 tablespoons baking powder
½ cup sugar
½ teaspoon cinnamon
½ cup butter, melted
½ cup milk
½ cup evaporated milk
1 teaspoon vanilla
2 eggs, beaten

Put graham crackers and nuts into a blender and blend until powdered (or grind in a grinder extra fine). Pour crumbs into a bowl, add remaining dry ingredients and mix well. Stir in butter, milk, evaporated milk, vanilla and eggs. Mix well and pour into an 8 x 8-inch loaf pan. Bake at 375° for 30 minutes or until a knife blade inserted in center comes out clean. Frost with CREAM CHEESE FROSTING (page 108). Serve in small pieces.

APPLE WHIP

¼ cup applesauce (page 40)
3 tablespoons heavy cream, whipped
1 or 2 drops vanilla

Fold applesauce and whipped cream together. Add vanilla. Chill slightly before serving.

PRUNE WHIP I

¾ cup stewed, sieved prunes
2 beaten egg whites
3 tablespoons sugar

Stew about 2 cups of dried prunes until tender. Put through a sieve. Add sugar. Beat egg whites until very stiff and fold into the mixture. Pour into a greased pie dish and bake at 350° for 25 minutes.

PRUNE WHIP II

Whip 3 tablespoons heavy cream and combine with ¼ cup chopped stewed prunes and a drop or two of vanilla.

FRUIT CHEESE

1 tablespoon cream cheese
2 teaspoons apple, pear or peach butter

Combine ingredients. Stir together until smooth.

Finger Foods

As soon as your baby is able to hold things to eat and shows interest in chewing them, start offering small pieces of fruits and vegetables. Be careful not to offer bits that the baby might choke on or inhale. Try sections of orange, grapefruit or even lemon; slices of apple, pear, peach or banana; pieces of celery, carrot, turnip, or potato. Try a pickle or slices of pitted ripe olives.

A WAY WITH APPLE

Core a firm apple. Cut slices about ½-inch wide crosswise and peel them. These doughnut-shaped slices can be held by even a young baby. Makes a tasty teething ring.

CARROT TEETHER

Bore a hole crosswise in a fat, firm carrot about an inch from the top. Thread it with a heavy cord and hang it around the baby's neck. Do not use this for babies with teeth because they may bite off chunks and swallow them without chewing.

BEEF JERKY

1 flank steak

Marinade:

½ cup soy sauce
¼ cup catsup
½ cup honey

Trim fat off flank steak. Chill in freezer for 10 minutes. Lay steak on chopping board and cut with sharp knife into very thin slices cutting with the grain. Marinate overnight. Put foil on lower oven rack to catch drips. Remove strips of meat from marinade and lay across grids of upper oven rack. Bake 150° for 2 to 3 hours or until very dry. Take out. Cut into 4-inch lengths. Store in tightly-closed glass jar. Good for snacks.

BUTTERED SCALLOPS

Cut up several medium-sized scallops and sauté in butter until tender. Add salt to taste and a drop or two of fresh lemon juice if the baby likes it.

SMALL-FRY FISH CUBES

1 filet of any firm-fleshed fish
 (cod, bass, halibut, haddock)
1 egg
3 tablespoons evaporated milk
½ cup flour

Cut the raw fish into bite-size cubes. Mix egg and milk together in a small bowl. Put the flour into a second small bowl. Roll the fish cubes in the flour, then in the egg mixture, then in the flour again. Place the cubes on a small cookie sheet or baking pan. Bake at 375° for 10 minutes. Remove, cool slightly and serve.

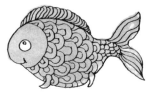

HOT DOGS & COLD CUTS

Warm an all-beef hot dog in boiling water for a few minutes. Cut in half crosswise, then in quarters lengthwise. Skin the sections. Offer an array of cold cuts and let the baby pick and choose.

LAMB KIDNEY

Wash, peel and slice open lengthwise a couple of lamb kidneys. Cut out all the white membrane. Fry quickly in a little butter or broil until nicely browned. Take out and cool. These are a nice size and shape for the baby to hold.

BONES

Offer your baby a chicken drumstick or a pork or lamb sparerib bone to bite, chew or suck.

DRIED FRUIT

Fill a little bowl full of bits of dried apricot, apple, pear, pitted prune and a few raisins.

SHELLFISH

Cut cooked shrimp, lobster or crab meat into bits to pick up and eat.

MEAT

Cut cooked tender meat into shreds for your baby to pick up and eat.

CHEESE

Cut little square sticks from any firm cheese. If you want to offer less cheese, cut finger-length pieces of bread from one slice, put very thin slices of cheese on top and broil until the cheese is melted. Cool and serve.

COLD BEAN CUP

Fill a cup half full of cooked beans (kidney, lima, pink, garbanzo, navy, etc.) and let the baby pick and choose.

MACARONI

Cook a handful of macaroni of various shapes (shell, elbow, rings etc.) in boiling water until tender. Drain, add a bit of butter or a sprinkle of grated cheese and serve.

SWEET POTATO STICKS

1 large sweet potato, cut into ½-inch sticks
½ teaspoon salt
1 cup dry pre-cooked baby cereal
1 egg, beaten lightly with 1 tablespoon water
  Oil for browning (1 tablespoon oil
  plus 1 tablespoon butter)

Boil sticks in salted water until just tender. Drain. Put cereal in one bowl and egg mixture in another. Roll sticks in cereal, then egg, then in cereal again. Brown quickly in hot oil and butter. Drain on absorbent paper. Serve warm.

BREAKFAST SCRAMBLE

1 egg, beaten
1 slice bread, cubed
1 slice bacon, chopped

Fry bacon in small frying pan until crisp. Add bread and fry until slightly brown. Pour egg on top of bread and stir with a fork until egg is cooked. Can be eaten hot or cold.

BANANA SAUTÉ

Sauté ½-inch thick slices of banana in butter until lightly browned. Remove from pan, dust lightly with cinnamon and allow to cool sufficiently before serving.

LANA'S BANANAS

Peel a banana and cut it into slices. Spread half the slices with peanut butter and top with the other half of the slices to make tiny sandwiches.

TINY SANDWICHES

Butter thin slices of bread and spread with minced meat or peanut butter, or mashed avocado, potato or baked beans. Top slices with another buttered slice of bread, trim crusts, cut into quarters. Make sure the bread slices are thin and that the sandwiches stick together. Try these fillings too:

Asparagus Tips & Lemon Juice: Mash a few cooked asparagus tips. Add a few drops of lemon juice and a few grains of salt. Spread on thin slices of brown bread.

Sardines & Cream Cheese: Mash ¼ pound of cream cheese with a fork. Add 2 tablespoons of lemon juice. Mash 1 can of sardines and mix with cheese. Spread on thin slices of dark bread.

PIZZA BAMBINO

Cut a round the size of an English muffin out of a slice of bread and spread it with tomato catsup. Add a generous sprinkling of cooked ground beef or pork sausage. Top with a slice of Monterey Jack or Mozzarella cheese. Put under the broiler and broil until the cheese is bubbly. Cut into small wedges and serve. Can be served hot or cold.

TOASTED CHEESE & BACON SQUARES

¼ pound cheddar cheese
2 slices bacon
1 tablespoon chopped onion
6 slices bread

Dice cheese and bacon. Add onion and put through a grinder. Spread slices of bread with mixture. Broil until bacon is cooked and cheese is melted and slightly brown. Remove from broiler, cut slices into quarters. Serve warm but not hot. This mixture can be kept in the refrigerator for up to a week and used a little at a time.

CHINESE SHRIMP TOAST

1 chicken liver, chopped
1 teaspoon butter
1 slice of bread
1 small cooked shrimp, chopped
Wheat germ for topping

Brown chicken liver in butter. Remove from heat and mash with a fork. Cut crusts off bread and cut into quarters. Spread each piece with chicken liver and add a layer of shrimp. Sprinkle with wheat germ. Broil 2 minutes.

LIVER BALLS

1 strip bacon
2 or 3 chicken livers

Fry bacon until crisp. Cool and break into bits. Crush it on a board with the bottom of a glass. Fry chicken livers in the bacon fat for a few minutes until they are nicely browned but still soft. Mash livers with a fork and mix in bacon. Shape into small balls about ½-inch in diameter. For variety add 1 tablespoon minced cooked beets.

CHEESE PUFFS

5 ounces water
½ stick butter (2 ounces)
  Scant ½ cup flour
2 eggs
2 ounces cheddar cheese, grated

Boil water, add butter and stir until butter is melted. Remove from heat and quickly beat in the flour. Let cool for 5 minutes. Add eggs, one at a time, beating until mixture is glossy. Add cheese and blend. Drop from a teaspoon onto a buttered cookie sheet. Bake at 375° for 25 minutes. Makes 2 dozen.

MINI MONTE CRISTO

1 thin slice soft bread, buttered
 Ham, thinly sliced
 Mild cheese, thinly sliced
1 egg, beaten
1 teaspoon milk

Trim crusts off bread and cut slice in half lengthwise. Cover one piece (buttered side) with ham. Add cheese. Top with bread and cut in half. Mix egg and milk. Dip both sides of sandwiches into the egg mixture. Remove sandwiches to a warm, buttered frying pan. Cook, covered, over low to moderate heat until brown on one side. Turn and brown the other side. Cook slowly so the cheese will melt. When done, cut sandwiches in half again for easier handling. Allow to cool slightly before serving.

MINIATURE MEAT BALLS

½ pound ground chuck
1 small egg
1½ teaspoons cornstarch
3 tablespoons soy sauce
1 teaspoon finely minced celery
1 teaspoon finely minced onion
1 quart water for cooking

Mix all ingredients except water thoroughly and shape into tiny meat-balls. Bring water to a boil. Drop meatballs into boiling water. Simmer uncovered for 20 minutes. Cool.

Advanced Gourmets
(nine months or more)

PETITE VICHYSSOISE

1 potato, peeled and cubed
1 carrot, peeled, sliced
1 leek, washed and sliced (white part only)
1 tablespoon butter or margarine
1½ cups chicken broth or 1 can (13¾-oz.)
   chicken broth
   Salt, pepper, nutmeg
¼ cup half-and-half

Cook potato and carrot in boiling, salted water to cover until tender. Drain. Melt butter in saucepan. Sauté leek until limp. Add half of broth and simmer until tender. Drain, reserving broth. Put carrots, potatoes and leek through a sieve or into the blender with all the broth. Add salt, pepper and nutmeg to taste. Blend. Chill. Just before serving mix half-and-half with the chilled mixture and blend.

GREAT-GRANDMA'S VEAL SOUP

    1 veal knuckle bone with meat
    2 quarts water
    2 teaspoons salt

Cook slowly for two hours and add:

    1 tablespoon rice
    1 cup chopped celery

Cook ½ hour longer. Make these dumplings:

    2 cups soft white bread crumbs
    1 egg
    2 tablespoons butter
      Salt and pepper

Moisten with broth to form balls 1-inch in diameter. Drop balls into soup. Cover and simmer 5 minutes.

CLAM SOUP

½ cup milk
2 tablespoons canned minced clams
2 tablespoons minced clam juice
¼ teaspoon butter
  Minced parsley (optional)
  Oyster crackers

Warm milk, clams and clam juice slowly. Do not allow to boil. Simmer for about 10 minutes so that flavors blend. Stir in butter and parsley. Float crackers on top.

BROILED SHRIMP

6 medium-sized fresh shrimp
  Butter or oil
  Soy sauce
  Garlic Salt
  Lemon juice

Wash, peel and de-vein shrimp. Place on a foil broiling pan which has a few dots of butter or drops of oil spread on it to prevent sticking. Season with sprinkles of soy sauce, garlic salt and lemon juice. Put under the broiler and broil for 1 minute. Chop or serve whole.

BELL PEPPERS & ONION

Equal amounts of:
> Green and red bell peppers,
>> cut lengthwise in thin strips
>
> Sweet yellow onion, sliced thin

Sauté in one tablespoon of oil, stirring constantly until peppers are soft. Serve strips to babies who like to eat with their hands. Chop fine or puree with a little vegetable oil for younger babies.

EGGS FLORENTINE

1 egg
½ cup chopped cooked spinach
Parmesan cheese

Poach egg. Make a hollow in the spinach with the back of a spoon and place the egg in it. Sprinkle with cheese.

SMILING SUN OMELET

1 egg
1 tablespoon butter
1 tablespoon milk
1 dried apricot
1 thin carrot stick
2 raisins

Break the egg into a small bowl. Add milk and beat with a fork until fluffy. Melt butter in a 6-inch frying pan. Pour the mixture into the pan and cook on low heat until set. Remove and decorate: Use raisins for eyes, apricot for nose, carrot for mouth.

SPANISH OMELET

2 tablespoons minced onion
2 teaspoons minced bell pepper
Butter
1 tablespoon chopped tomato
1 egg, beaten
2 teaspoons milk
Salt

Sauté onion and pepper lightly in butter. Add tomato and cook for one minute longer over low heat. Mix egg and milk together. Add dash of salt. Combine egg and vegetable mixture and puree. Pour into well-buttered 6-inch frying pan. Cook over low heat until egg begins to set around edges. Cover and continue cooking slowly until egg is done.

PETITS POTS

1 small can (7½-oz.) each of:
  green beans, petits pois, whole kernel corn
½ cup heavy cream
2 ounces of butter

Mix vegetables and cream together. Put into six custard cups, dot with butter and bake at 350° for 20 minutes.

ZUCCHINI FRITATAS

¾ cup finely chopped zucchini
¼ cup powdered milk
1 egg
½ cup baby oatmeal (pre-cooked)
  Dash of salt
2 tablespoons vegetable oil

Mix ingredients in a bowl. Drop from a tablespoon into a lightly greased frying pan. Fry until lightly browned on both sides. Remove with slotted spoon and drain on absorbent paper.

SUKIYAKI

3 tablespoons hot water
1 teaspoon soy sauce
½ teaspoon sugar
2 tablespoons any tender raw beef,
  sliced thin and then cut in small pieces
½ teaspoon vegetable oil
4 tablespoons mixed chopped
  vegetables (celery, mushrooms,
  scallions, spinach, chard, cabbage or
  fresh bean sprouts in any combination)

Combine water, soy sauce and sugar in a cup and set aside. In a heavy pan sauté meat quickly in oil. Lower heat, add chopped vegetables and soy sauce mixture and stir. Simmer slowly until vegetables are barely tender. Add more sauce if desired. Serve with boiled rice.

Boiled rice:
1 cup long grain rice
1½ cups water
  Pinch of salt

Wash the rice thoroughly several times in cold water and drain off starchy water. Put into heavy pot (with tight-fitting lid) with the 1½ cups water and salt. Cover pot and bring to boiling. Boil 3 minutes, then turn heat down to lowest point and cook 15 minutes.

GIYOZA

(Japanese Dumplings)

Dough:

    1 package of prepared won ton skins

Filling:

    ¼ pound ground beef or pork
    1 tablespoon finely chopped onion
    2 tablespoons sesame or peanut oil
    1 teaspoon soy sauce
      Pinch of garlic powder

Cook meat. Drain off excess fat. Mix with rest of ingredients. Put a teaspoonful of filling in the center of each square of dough. Seal edges of each skin or wrapper by moistening edges with water, and pressing firmly together. Put oil in frying pan and heat until hot. Brown dumplings on both sides. Add 2 tablespoons of water to the pan, cover tightly and steam for 2 minutes.

LITTLE CHICKEN LEGS

6 chicken wings
½ cup soy sauce
½ teaspoon garlic salt
  Juice of 1 lemon

Cut off wing tips, then cut the two remaining parts apart at the joint. Mix rest of ingredients for a basting sauce. Put the chicken pieces (which look like little chicken legs) in a shallow pan and baste well. Bake about 45 minutes at 350° turning once.

BABY BLANQUETTE

1 thin veal scallop,
  ground or chopped fine
1 teaspoon oil
1 small carrot, sliced
1 green onion, chopped (optional)
3 tablespoons cream of mushroom soup
2 tablespoons evaporated milk
  Pinch of thyme

Brown veal in oil. Cook carrot and onion until tender in water to cover. Mix soup, milk and thyme together in a sauce pan. Add meat and vegetables. Heat until warm.

CHINESE DINNER

Many Chinese foods make wonderful baby foods and can be picked up easily and eaten by the baby. Chop up an assortment of the following:

> Mushrooms
> Bean sprouts
> Bamboo shoots
> Chinese celery
> Sliced carrot
> Pineapple chunks
> Snow peas
> Tiny shrimp
> Thin strips of flank steak, cut against the grain

Brown the meat if you use steak. Fry or steam the vegetables until they are tender. Cook shrimp if fresh, warm if canned. Use different combinations and let the baby pick and choose. Add a few drops of soy sauce for a non-sweet taste or the following sweet-and-sour sauce.

> Sauce:
> ¼ cup vinegar
> ¼ cup brown sugar
> ¼ cup catsup
> ¼ cup water
> 1 teaspoon cornstarch mixed with
> 1 tablespoon water

Combine ingredients except for cornstarch and bring to a boil. Add cornstarch gradually and cook stirring constantly until thick. Mix with other ingredients.

MINI MOUSSAKA

1 small eggplant, cut into 1½-inch thick slices
Slices of Monterey Jack or Mozzarella cheese
3 tablespoons cottage cheese
1½ cups tomato sauce (with or without meat)

Steam eggplant in small amount of water until tender, and drain. Put half of the tomato sauce into the bottom of a baking dish. Add a layer of eggplant slices, a layer of cottage cheese, and a layer of Monterey Jack cheese. Pour remaining sauce on top. Bake at 350° until cheese is melted. Bake in an aluminum foil pan and freeze remainder for later use.

SPINACH MEAT PIE

3 cups chopped, raw spinach leaves
1½ tablespoons cooked, ground meat
Grated Jack or Swiss cheese
Fine bread crumbs

Wash spinach thoroughly in several waters. Boil in small amount of water until tender. Drain well, then puree. Put half of the spinach in a small buttered casserole. Spread meat on top and cover with the rest of the spinach. Sprinkle with cheese and bread crumbs. Dot with butter. Bake about 5 minutes in 350° oven.

BEEF & KIDNEY PIE

2 tablespoons butter
1 lamb or veal kidney, chopped
1 mushroom, chopped
1 green onion, chopped
¼ pound steak, chopped
2 tablespoons flour
½ cup mashed potato
2 tablespoons milk
1 teaspoon butter

Remove all white membrane from kidney. Melt butter in frying pan. Brown kidney and mushroom. Add onion. Put flour into a small paper bag, add steak and shake well. Add floured steak to pan and brown. Spoon mixture into small casserole. Add ¼ cup water to frying pan, stir to make a thin gravy and pour over meat mixture. Heat milk and butter and mix with mashed potato. Spread potato on top of pie. Bake at 350° for 20 minutes.

CHICKEN RICE PILAF

¼ cup uncooked long grain white rice
2 teaspoons minced celery
½ teaspoon minced scallion
1 teaspoon olive oil
½ cup chicken broth
2 tablespoons chopped chicken
Salt to taste

Wash rice thoroughly in cold water and drain. Sauté celery and scallion lightly in olive oil. Add rice and stir until it is coated with oil. Add chicken broth, chopped chicken and salt. Bring to a boil. Turn down heat, cover and cook over very low heat until rice is tender and broth has been absorbed (15 to 20 minutes).

CHEESE SOUFFLÉ WITH BACON

1 tablespoon butter
1 tablespoon flour
⅓ cup scalded milk
2 eggs, separated
¼ cup grated cheddar cheese
Pinch of salt
Crumbled bacon bits

Melt butter in the top of a double boiler. Blend in flour. Add milk gradually, stirring until smooth. Remove. Beat egg yolks until light and add to milk and flour mixture. Beat egg whites until stiff and fold in lightly. Pour into greased casserole. Bake at 375° until soufflé puffs up and is lightly browned on top (20 to 30 minutes). Serve at once sprinkled with crisp-cooked bacon bits.

AFRICAN BABOTEE

2 tablespoons butter or margarine
1 small onion, chopped
1 pound ground beef or lamb
1 slice bread, soaked in milk and drained
1 teaspoon salt
½ teaspoon curry powder
 Juice of 1 lemon
½ cup cooked apricot pulp
2 beaten eggs
1 cup milk

Sauté onion in melted butter until yellow. Add meat and brown. Remove from heat. Put bread, meat, onion, salt, curry powder, lemon juice and apricot pulp into a bowl and mix well. Add eggs to milk and stir well. Stir ½ the milk mixture into the meat mixture. Put into greased casserole (or 6 custard cups). Bake at 350° for 20 minutes. Pour remaining milk mixture over the top. Return to oven and bake 20 minutes more or until custard is set. Wrap extra portions in foil and freeze for later use. When ready to use, heat in 400° oven for 30 minutes.

CREAMY HADDOCK FILET

½ pound haddock filet
1 cup cream sauce made with:
    2 tablespoons butter
    2 tablespoons flour
    1 cup milk

Simmer haddock until tender in water to cover. Drain and cool. Carefully remove bones, flake fish, then put into a blender. Melt butter in top of double boiler. Add flour, stirring constantly. Remove from heat and stir in milk. Return to heat and cook and stir until thick. Add sauce to blender and blend for just a few seconds. (If you do not have a blender, shred cooked fish very fine and combine with sauce.) Serve as is or put into a baking dish, sprinkle with bread crumbs and bake for 20 minutes at 350.°

BAKED FISH

1 small filet of any firm, white fish
½ teaspoon garlic powder
2 tablespoons soy sauce
   Butter

Cut a piece of aluminum foil about 8 inches square. Lay filet on foil. Sprinkle with garlic powder and soy sauce. Dot with butter. Bring foil up around filet and form a tight package. Put package on an oven-proof dish and bake for 20 to 30 minutes at 325.°

SAVORY RICOTTA TARTS

Pastry:

 2 tablespoons butter
 ¼ cup flour

Filling:

 3 tablespoons ricotta cheese
 1 tablespoon chopped, smoked salmon
 1 egg
 1 slice Monterey Jack cheese
 Salt and pepper to taste

Melt the butter in a small pan and pour into the flour. Mix with a fork until a dough is formed. Press dough with fingertips into 2 tart tins or into a 4-inch in diameter pie pan. Mix all the filling ingredients except cheese slice. Pour filling into tins and lay cheese slice on top. Bake at 400° for 15 minutes for tarts, or 30 minutes for single pie.

SWEET RICOTTA TARTS: Add 1 teaspoon of sugar to the pastry. Use a filling made from: 1½ tablespoons fruit puree, 2 tablespoons ricotta cheese and 1 egg. Follow same procedure as that for Savory Tarts.

CHEESE LOGS

1½ cups flour
¼ pound butter
1 cup grated cheddar cheese
½ cup nuts, powdered
1 egg yolk

Work butter into flour with your fingertips to consistency of coarse meal. Add rest of ingredients and mix until you have a firm, dry dough. If it is too dry, add a tablespoon of water. Take a piece of dough and roll it between your hands until you form a log about 3 inches long and ½-inch in diameter. Place on greased cookie sheet and bake at 375° for 12 minutes or until slightly brown. Serve logs plain or make a mixture of equal amounts of cream cheese and strawberry jam to spread on them. Makes about 2 dozen cookies.

CRÊPES

½ cup milk
1 egg
4 teaspoons flour
Pinch of salt
2 teaspoons melted butter or margarine

Spread with any of these:

Jam or jelly
Cinnamon and sugar
Sugar and lemon juice
Mashed leftover vegetables, mixed
with a little milk
Grated cheese
Any fruit puree

Whisk a little of the milk and the egg together in a mixing bowl. Add flour, salt and remaining milk. Whisk well. Let rest a few minutes. Melt butter in small frying pan. Add to batter and stir. Make thin pancakes with spoonsful of batter. Fry until light brown, turning once. Remove and spread immediately with any of the suggested spreads. Roll up loosely and serve.

PUMPKIN-GINGER CAKE

¾ cup molasses
¼ cup oil
½ cup yogurt
3 eggs
⅔ cup canned pumpkin
1¾ cups flour
½ teaspoon salt
½ teaspoon ginger
⅓ cup wheat germ
½ teaspoon pumpkin pie spice

Put molasses, oil and yogurt into mixing bowl. Beat eggs and add. Add pumpkin. Sift flour, salt, ginger and pumpkin pie spice together and add to pumpkin mixture. Add wheat germ and mix well. Bake in a greased 8x12-inch pan at 350° for 50 minutes. Cut into squares.

HONEY-MOLASSES COOKIES

½ cup honey
½ cup lard or other shortening
⅓ cup molasses
½ teaspoon vanilla
1 teaspoon baking soda (dissolved
      in ¼ cup warm water)
2 cups unbleached flour
   Pinch of salt

Preheat oven to 375.° Combine all ingredients except 1 cup flour. Beat until smooth. Add remaining flour ½ cup at a time. Drop from a teaspoon onto a greased cookie sheet. Press flat with the bottom of a glass which has been dipped in flour. Bake for 12 minutes. Makes about 30 cookies.

Frosting:
Heat three tablespoons of cream or milk until hot. Remove from heat and stir in 2 cups of powdered sugar. Blend until creamy. Add 2 teaspoons vanilla and blend. If too thin, add more sugar. If too thick, add more milk.

CARROT DROP COOKIES

- 1 stick butter
- ⅓ cup sugar
- 1 egg
- 1½ cups flour
- ½ cup high protein baby cereal
- ½ teaspoon baking powder
- ½ teaspoon salt
- ½ teaspoon cinnamon
- 1 cup pureed carrots
- ½ cup nuts, powdered
- ½ cup currants (optional)

Cream butter and sugar together until light. Add egg and beat well. Sift dry ingredients together and add alternately with carrot puree. Mix thoroughly. Add nuts and currants. Drop by spoonfuls onto greased cookie sheet. Bake about 10 minutes at 375.º Makes about 3 dozen soft cookies.

BANANA SMOOTHIE

½ banana, peeled, frozen
  Milk
½ teaspoon vanilla
1 teaspoon honey

Slice the frozen banana into a blender. Pour in enough milk to cover. Add vanilla and honey. Blend until smooth and frothy. For children over a year old, frozen strawberries may be added or substituted.

APRICOT MOUSSE

1 cup cooked, strained apricots
½ cup heavy cream, whipped
2 tablespoons powdered sugar
  Grated semi-sweet chocolate for topping

Blend sugar into whipped cream. Fold cream into apricots. Spoon into serving dish, top with chocolate and chill.

GRANDMA'S CREAMY RICE

1 quart milk
½ cup uncooked rice
¼ teaspoon salt
¼ cup sugar
1 egg yolk, mixed with 1 tablespoon water
1 teaspoon vanilla

Put milk, rice and salt into heavy saucepan. Bring to a boil. Turn down heat and cook until mixture thickens, stirring frequently. (This takes about 2 hours.) Add sugar and diluted egg yolk. Stir well. Cook for another 5 minutes. Remove from fire. Stir in vanilla. Serve warm or cold.

BLUEBERRY PUDDING

½ cup bread crumbs
1 tablespoon butter
1 cup hot milk
⅛ cup sugar
1 egg, beaten lightly
   Pinch of salt
½ teaspoon vanilla
½ cup canned blueberries

Pour hot milk over crumbs and butter. Cool. Add remaining ingredients, mix well and pour into a medium-size baking dish. Bake at 325° for 45 minutes. Or, put into 3 or 4 baking cups and bake 30 minutes.

GREAT-GREAT-GRANDMA'S ICE CREAM

2 teaspoons sugar
1 beaten egg yolk
1 cup milk
1 beaten egg white
½ cup heavy cream, whipped
1 teaspoon vanilla
   Pinch of salt

Add sugar to beaten egg yolk. Scald milk. Add egg mixture to milk and boil until creamy and smooth. Remove from fire. Fold in beaten egg white. Let cool. Fold in whipped cream, vanilla and salt. Freeze in ice cube tray until mushy, then stir well. Return to freezer and freeze until solid.

FIRST BIRTHDAY CAKE

2 eggs
1 cup flour
1 teaspoon cinnamon
1 teaspoon baking powder
1 teaspoon soda
½ teaspoon salt
1 cup sugar
¾ cup oil
1½ cups finely grated carrots

Put eggs into mixing bowl and beat. Sift dry ingredients together and add. Add oil. Stir until well blended. Pour into a round 9-inch in diameter, or square 8 x 8-inch cake pan. Bake ½ hour at 350°

Cream Cheese Frosting:
½ box powdered sugar
3 ounces cream cheese
¼ stick butter
1 teaspoon vanilla

Beat all ingredients together until creamy. Frost cake.

HOT CHOCOLATE SUNDAE

1 cup powdered sugar
1 egg
¼ teaspoon salt
2 squares semi-sweet chocolate
2 tablespoons butter
  Cream for thinning

Put sugar, egg, salt and chocolate into pan and set over low heat. Stir until chocolate is dissolved. (Do not boil.) Add butter and stir thoroughly. Remove from heat and thin to desired consistency with cream. Serve hot over ice cream. Sauce can be refrigerated and reheated.

1-2-3 POPSICLES

1. Pour any natural unsweetened fruit juice into popsicle molds and freeze.
2. Put 2 pints of fresh or frozen strawberries into a blender and blend to liquid consistency. Pour into molds and freeze.
3. Mix 1 cup of strawberry puree with 1 cup of heavy cream. Add 1 tablespoon of vanilla and ¾ cup powdered sugar. Mix well. Pour into molds and freeze.

YOGURT POPSICLES

1 can (6-oz.) frozen orange juice concentrate
1 pint plain yogurt
1 teaspoon vanilla
⅓ cup wheat germ or granola, ground fine

Put all ingredients into mixing bowl and beat well with beater, or put into blender and puree. Pour into 3½-oz. plastic or paper cups. Stick a small plastic spoon into the middle of each popsicle. Freeze. After 5 hours, the popsicles will be the consistency of ice-cream. Frozen overnight the popsicles will be hard. Makes 7 popsicles.

STRAWBERRY SORBET

1 quart fresh or frozen strawberries
2 egg whites
½ cup sugar (optional)
¼ cup lemon juice

Wash strawberries and discard stems. (If you use frozen fruit, defrost, drain, puree and add enough juice to make 2 cups.) Beat egg whites to soft peaks. Put rest of ingredients into a blender and puree. Fold egg whites into puree. Cover and freeze until set. Remove from freezer, beat with electric beater to break up ice crystals. The mixture will become lighter and fluffier. Spoon the sherbet into small cups for individual servings or put into freezer container. Cover and freeze until hard. For PEACH SORBET substitute peaches for strawberries and follow the same procedure.

Baby Casseroles
(for the one-year-old)

A year-old baby should be able to eat most of the foods you eat, but the baby may be on a different schedule, so it is helpful to prepare some meals in advance. Little ready-to-eat casserole dishes can be frozen, stored and re-heated later. Each of these recipes makes approximately one 8-ounce casserole.

GOURMET GRAINS

½ cup cooked brown rice
¼ cup cooked wheatberries
¼ cup grated cheddar cheese
3 or 4 washed spinach or chard
 leaves, chopped
1 egg, beaten
 Pinch of garlic salt

Put all ingredients into a mixing bowl and mix thoroughly. Turn out into a small casserole. Bake uncovered for 15 to 20 minutes at 350°.

VEGETABLES & MACARONI

¼ cup cooked macaroni
½ cup canned vegetable soup
1 tablespoon finely grated Parmesan cheese

Put the macaroni into a small casserole. Pour the soup over it. Sprinkle the top with cheese. Bake at 350° for about 10 minutes.

ESCALLOPED CRAB

1 can (5½-oz.) crabmeat
2 tablespoons butter
1 cup milk
1 tablespoon leek soup mix
4 tablespoons cracker crumbs
2 tablespoons grated cheddar cheese
Salt and pepper to taste

Melt butter in a small saucepan. Add the flour and stir until blended. Remove from fire. Add milk slowly, beating constantly with a wire whisk. Return to fire and cook, stirring, until thickened. Add crabmeat and soup mix. If this is for a baby who does not like lumps, put the whole mixture into a blender and blend until smooth. Pour into a casserole and sprinkle with crumbs and cheese. Bake at 350° for 20 minutes or until brown and bubbly.

KEDGEREE

1 tablespoon chopped onion
2 tablespoons butter
1 egg, hard-cooked
¼ pound cooked, flaked fish
⅔ cup cooked rice
   Salt to taste

Sauté the onion in butter until soft. Separate the egg white from the yolk. Chop the egg white. Stir onion, fish, egg white and salt into the rice. Put into a buttered casserole. Crumble the egg yolk and sprinkle on top of fish mixture. Cover and heat in 350° oven for about 15 minutes.

SQUAW CORN

1 small can (8-oz.) yellow creamed corn
1 hot dog, sliced

Put creamed corn and hot dog slices into casserole. Stir. Bake uncovered in 350° oven until hot and bubbly.

SPAGHETTI

⅓ cup uncooked spaghetti, broken
   into small pieces
½ cup spaghetti sauce

Cook spaghetti in large amount of boiling water until tender. Drain. Put into small casserole. Mix with sauce. Bake at 350° for 15 minutes.

Sauce:
¼ cup chopped lean beef
1 tablespoon minced onion
1 can (8-oz.) tomato sauce
1 tablespoon grated carrot
¼ teaspoon dried basil
   Garlic salt and pepper to taste

Fry beef and onion in small frying pan until tender. Add rest of ingredients and simmer for 15 minutes.

EGGPLANT PARMIGIANA

¼ cup peeled, diced eggplant
¼ cup flour
¼ cup ground beef
1 egg, beaten
1 tablespoon minced onion
1 tablespoon tomato paste
2 tablespoons grated cheese
   Salt & pepper to taste

Put flour into a paper bag, add eggplant cubes and shake to coat them with flour. Saute meat and onion in a small amount of oil until brown. Remove meat and onion and reserve. Saute eggplant in oil (with a lump of butter added to the oil) until soft and brown. Combine ingredients and seasonings and put into small casserole. Bake uncovered for 15 to 20 minutes at 350.°

CHICKEN & RICE

½ stalk celery
½ carrot
1 small onion
½ cup cooked chopped chicken
¼ cup cooked rice
½ cup undiluted cream of celery soup

Chop vegetables and cook until tender in small amount of water. Drain. Combine with rest of ingredients. Spoon into casserole. Bake uncovered in 350° oven for ½ hour.

TURKEY TETRAZZINI

½ cup cooked, diced turkey (or chicken)
½ cup cooked macaroni
¼ cup cream of mushroom soup
1 tablespoon finely grated Parmesan cheese

Put turkey, macaroni and soup into a buttered casserole. Stir to mix. Sprinkle the top with the cheese. Bake at 350° for about 15 minutes.

CORNED BEEF

½ cup chopped cooked corned beef
¼ cup cream of mushroom soup
½ cup cooked thinly-sliced potato
1 small thinly-sliced onion

Combine ingredients. Spoon into casserole. Bake uncovered in 350° oven for ½ hour.

BEEF & SWEET POTATO

½ cup cooked thinly-sliced round steak
½ cup cooked mashed sweet potato
1 teaspoon brown sugar
Butter, salt and pepper to taste

Combine ingredients. Spoon into casserole. Bake covered in 350° oven for ½ hour.

Breads

If you have never baked bread you may be inspired to start baking real homemade breads for your baby—a good way to add nutrients to your baby's diet and to introduce a variety of wonderful flavors, aromas and textures that will add pleasure to your baby's meals.

HEALTH BREAD

(This bread has many vitamins and minerals lacking in commercial breads.)

1 package dry yeast
4 tablespoons lukewarm water
⅔ cup powdered milk
2 cups lukewarm water
2 teaspoons salt
2 tablespoons melted shortening
2 tablespoons molasses
2 tablespoons honey
½ cup wheat germ
4½ cups whole wheat flour

Dissolve yeast in 4 tablespoons lukewarm water. Dissolve powdered milk in 2 cups lukewarm water and put into large mixing bowl. Add salt, shortening, molasses and honey. Stir. Add yeast, wheat germ and flour. Let rise in warm place until doubled in bulk. Punch down and knead for 5 minutes. Form into loaves and put into 2 well-greased loaf tins. Cover with a thin cloth and set to rise in a warm place for 1 hour. Preheat oven to 375° and bake for 50 minutes.

SWEDISH RUSK

 1 package dry yeast
 ¼ cup warm water
 ⅔ cup lard or other shortening
 1 cup milk
 ½ teaspoon salt
 ½ cup sugar
 1⅓ cups rye flour
 3 cups unbleached white flour

Dissolve yeast in warm water. Melt lard, cool a bit and add milk. Cool until lukewarm. Put salt and sugar into a bowl. Add liquid, yeast and rye flour. Mix with a wooden spoon until smooth. Add white flour, reserving ¾ of a cup. Beat until smooth and form ball of dough. Cover and let rise in warm place until doubled in bulk. Add remaining flour. Turn dough out on a floured board and knead 5 minutes. Divide dough into 3 or 4 parts and shape into small loaves. Place on a cookie sheet and let rise 1 hour. Bake at 425° for 20 minutes or until light brown. Remove, cover and cool. Cut loaves lengthwise once, then cut sides into 1-inch thick slices. Place on a baking sheet and bake in a 200° oven until dry and light brown. It takes about 3 hours to dry the rusks.

RUSKS I

Slice stale bread into fingers. Leave plain or spread with honey or jam. Bake in 200° oven until thoroughly dry and crisp. Takes 5 to 6 hours.

RUSKS II

1 cup milk
2 tablespoons honey
1 egg
3 slices bread (rye, whole wheat
   or white)

Mix milk, honey and egg together in a shallow pan. Cut the bread into fingers and soak in milk mixture for ½ hour. Grease another shallow pan and transfer the rusks to it. Bake overnight in a 200° oven.

PETER'S CORN BREAD

¾ cup cornmeal
½ cup flour
¼ cup sugar
1 tablespoon baking powder
¾ teaspoon salt
½ cup whole-wheat flour
2 tablespoons sesame seeds
1 cup milk
1 egg
2 tablespoons oil

Sift cornmeal, flour, sugar, baking powder and salt together into a bowl. Mix in whole-wheat flour and sesame seeds. Add milk, egg and oil. Bake in an 8 x 8-inch pan at 425° for 20 minutes. This is a firm, not crumbly corn bread.

BALLOON BREAD

½ cup water
1 cup whole-wheat flour
½ teaspoon salt
1 teaspoon sugar
  Oil for frying

Mix dry ingredients with water to form dough. Toss onto a floured board and knead for a few minutes. Break off small pieces of dough and form into balls ½ to 1 inch in diameter. Pat or roll flat to about ¼" thickness. Heat an inch of oil in heavy pan until hot enough to deep fry. Drop dough disks into oil one at a time. To make them balloon, you must press them to the bottom of the pan with the back of a wooden spoon and keep pressing them until they puff up. Fry a few seconds on each side until lightly browned. Remove with slotted spoon. Drain on paper towels.

LITTLE WHOLE-WHEAT BISCUITS

½ cup whole-wheat flour
½ cup unbleached white flour
1½ teaspoons baking powder
¼ teaspoon salt
1 teaspoon sugar
2 tablespoons lard or other shortening
½ cup milk

Sift dry ingredients together into a bowl. Work lard in with fingertips. Stir in milk to make a soft dough. Turn out onto a floured board and knead 1 minute. Pat into a smooth round about 1½ inches thick. Cut out with a shot glass or shape into tiny balls with your hands and then flatten balls to 1½-inch thickness. Bake at 450° for 15 minutes or until nicely browned.

BAKING POWDER BISCUITS

2 cups sifted all-purpose flour
3 teaspoons baking powder
¾ teaspoon salt
¼ cup vegetable shortening
⅔ cup milk

Combine flour, baking powder, salt and shortening. Using your fingertips, blend the mixture until it is the consistency of cornmeal. Stir in milk to make a soft dough. Turn out onto a lightly floured surface. Knead gently into a ball. Roll out to ½-inch thickness. Use a shot glass to cut out small biscuits. Place the biscuits on a greased pan close together and bake in 450° oven until lightly browned.

PRETZELS

1 square fresh or 1 package of dry yeast
Pinch of salt
½ teaspoon sugar
1¼ cups lukewarm water
2 to 3 cups unbleached white flour
1 cup whole-wheat flour
1 egg, beaten with 1 tablespoon water

Put crumbled yeast, salt and sugar into water and let stand about an hour. Add flour and stir until dough is formed. Toss dough onto a floured board and knead for 4 or 5 minutes. Put into a greased bowl, cover and let rise in warm place until double in bulk. Pinch off pieces of dough, roll into long narrow rolls and form pretzel shapes. Put pretzels on cookie sheet. Cover and let rise about 10 minutes. Brush with egg mixture. Bake 10 to 20 minutes (depending on size) at 375.°

OATMEAL CRACKERS

Mix 2 cups of oatmeal with 1½ cups of cold water. Work into a mass with a spoon. Place on a board well-covered with dry oatmeal. Make as compact as possible. Roll out carefully to about ⅛ of an inch. Cut in 2-inch squares with a knife. Bake at 250° for about 2 hours or until hard and crisp. These crackers are good for teething. They will keep for weeks in an airtight container. Makes 2 dozen crackers.

MARY FISK, who wrote the *Baby Gourmet Cookbook,* became interested in child nutrition when her own baby refused to eat commercially prepared baby food. When she failed to find a satisfactory guide for planning and preparing baby food at home, she decided to write one of her own. She developed her own techniques for researching and testing recipes, consulted nutritionists and friends, and this collection of recipes is the result of that effort.

Educated at Radcliffe College, San Diego State University and the University of California, San Diego, Graduate School, she is presently a research associate in Marine Geology at Scripps Institution of Oceanography, La Jolla. She lives in nearby Del Mar, California.

SUSAN PERL, who illustrated the *Baby Gourmet Cookbook,* lives in New York city where she has lived since 1939 when she arrived in this country from Austria with her family. She started out as a fashion illustrator when she was barely a teen-ager, and switched to free-lance art work in 1957. Since that time she has illustrated more than fifty children's books and a number of adult books. Her work appears regularly in magazines and newspapers and her bright-haired, freckle-faced children with their menagerie of loveable, funny animals, birds and bugs are familiar to most readers.